# Gorillas

## Patricia Kendell

RAINTREE
STECK-VAUGHN
PUBLISHERS

A Harcourt Company

Austin   New York
www.raintreesteckvaughn.com

# Alligators   Chimpanzees   Dolphins
# Elephants   Gorillas   Grizzly Bears
# Leopards   Lions   Pandas
# Polar Bears   Sharks   Tigers

Published by Raintree Steck-Vaughn Publishers, an imprint of Steck-Vaughn Company

**Library of Congress Cataloging-in-Publication Data available upon request**

ISBN 0-7398-5497-6

Printed in Hong Kong. Bound in the United States.

1 2 3 4 5 6 7 8 9 0 LB 06 05 04 03 02

Photograph acknowledgments:
Bruce Coleman 3 (second & third), 4, 9, 15, 17, 24; FLPA 12 (Minden Pictures), 13 (T Whittaker), 19 (Michael Gore), 3 (fourth), 25 (Jurgen & Christine Sohns), 26 (Brake/Sunset); NHPA 28 (Martin Harvey), 11, 16, 20 (Steve Robinson), 18 (Nigel J Dennis);Oxford Scientific Films 5 (Mike Birkhead), 10 (Konrad Wothe), 29 (Clive Bromhall);Science Photo Library 3 (first), 14, 21 (Tom McHugh), 22 (Tim Davis);Still Pictures 1, 8, 23, 32 (Michel Gunther), 7 (John Cancalosi), 27 (Paul Harrison); WWF  D Lawson 6.

# Contents

# Where Gorillas Live

Gorillas live in parts of Africa. Some live in the **tropical forests** of western and eastern Africa.

Other members of the gorilla family live in the misty mountain forests of central Africa. There are very few of these gorillas left in the wild.

# Baby Gorillas

A newly born gorilla is tiny and helpless.
The baby drinks milk from its mother.

Gorilla babies cling to their mother's chest,
where they feel safe and warm. They do this
until they are about 10 weeks old.

# Looking After the Babies

Gorilla mothers are very gentle and loving. They teach their babies which leaves and fruits are good to eat.

A baby gorilla will ride on its mother's back even
after it learns to walk alone. It will do this until it
is two and a half years old.

# Family Life

The babies live with their mothers in
a family group in their **home range**.
This group is led by a male **silverback**.

Gorillas are very friendly and live together peacefully.

# Growing Up

As the babies grow bigger they play games with each other. They practice the skills they will need when they grow up.

When this male gorilla is 12 years old, he will leave the group. Then he will find a **mate** and start a new family group of his own.

# Finding Food

Gorillas eat mainly
bamboo shoots, fruits,
leaves, and roots. They
sometimes travel long
distances to find food.

In the mountain forests, there is often plenty
of food. This means that these gorillas do not
need to travel far to find food.

# Eating

Gorillas sit down to eat. They reach out for leaves and fruit with their long arms. Sometimes they climb trees to find food, grasping the branches with their toes.

They pick stems, leaves, and berries using their fingers and thumbs.

# Rest and sleep

After a good meal, the gorillas relax
for a few hours before feeding again.

As the sun goes down, each gorilla makes a nest
of leafy stems. They sleep here until morning.

# Keeping Clean and Warm

Gorillas like being together and helping each other to keep clean. They groom each other's fur to get rid of insects and dirt. This mother is cleaning her baby.

Mountain gorillas have thick fur that keeps them warm even in the cold rain.

# Gentle giants

Adult males are large and heavy.
They can look very fierce.

Silverbacks will stand and beat their chests if they feel threatened, or to warn the **troop** of danger. Real fights are rare as gorillas prefer a quiet life.

# Threats

Gorillas are in great danger. Their forest homes are being cut down so people can grow food and raise their animals.

Local people have always eaten gorilla meat.
**Park rangers** try to stop this from happening.

# Gorillas in Danger

These people are helping a gorilla that
has fallen into a trap.

Park rangers will try to find the family group of an **orphan** baby. Sadly, some baby gorillas are captured by **smugglers** and end up in zoos.

# Helping Gorillas to Survive

Some people in Africa are working together to set up **protected areas** in the forest, where the gorillas can live safely. These park guides are watching the gorillas.

8

Local people can earn money from the tourists who
come to see the gorillas. This means a better future
for gorillas and people.

# Further Information

## ORGANIZATIONS TO CONTACT

**World Wildlife Fund**
1250 24th Street, NW
P.O. Box 97180
Washington, D.C. 20077-7180

**The Wildlife Society**
5410 Grosveenor Lane
Bethesda, MD 20814

**Care for the Wild**
P.O. Box 46250
Madison, WI 53744-6250

## BOOKS

Horton, Casey. *Apes (Endangered!)*. Chicago, IL: Benchmark Books, 1996.

Simon, Seymour. *Gorillas*. New York: Harper Collins Children's Books, 2000.

Weber, Bill and Vedder, Amy. *In the Kingdom of Gorillas: Fragile Species in a Dangerous Land*. New York: Simon and Schuster, 2001.

Wexo, John Bonnett. *Gorillas*. Poway, CA: Wildlife Education Ltd., 2000.

# Glossary

## WEBSITES

Most young children will need adult help when visiting websites. Those listed have child-friendly pages to bookmark.

http://www.koko.org/kidsclub
This site features the story of Koko, a gorilla born in a zoo. There are interesting facts about gorillas and their natural habitat.

http://www.gorilla-haven.org/
A site that promotes education about gorilla conservation in the wild as well as in zoos. There are pages for children with stories about particular gorillas and links to other sites.

http://www.nationalgeographic.com/kids
Look here for fun facts, photographs and video sequences about mountain gorillas.

home range – (HOME RAYNJ) the area where a gorilla troop lives and finds food.

mate – (MATE) a female gorilla who a male gorilla has babies with.

orphan – (OR-fuhn) an animal or person whose parents have both died.

protected areas – (pruh-TEK-tid AIR-ee-uhz) special places where wild animals are safe and free.

silverback – (SIL-ver-BAK) the name given to a male gorilla because of its silver-tipped fur.

smugglers – (SMUHG-uhl-urz) people who secretly take animals from the wild.

troop – (TROOP) a family group of gorillas.

tropical forests – (TROP-uh-kuhl-FOR istz) forests in places where it is very hot and wet.

# Index

32